Elaine Mintzer

Natural Selections

BOMBSHELTER PRESS
Los Angeles / 2005

Copyright © 2005 by Elaine Mintzer
All rights reserved

Other than brief quotations in a review, no part of this book may be reproduced without written permission of the publisher or copyright holder.

ISBN: 0-941017-26-5

Some of the poems have appeared in *ONTHEBUS*, *Rattle*, *Spillway*, *cold-drill*, *Shiela-Na-Gig*, and *13 Los Angeles Poets*.

A Black Mission Fig Press book
Bombshelter Press
www.bombshelterpress.com
books@bombshelterpress.com
PO Box 481266 Bicentennial Station
Los Angeles, California 90048 USA

Printed in the United States of America

Cover illustration by Carol Hargraves Upston
Author photograph by Rose Upston
Leaf photograph by Elaine Mintzer
Layout & Design: Alan Berman

Elaine Mintzer

Natural Selections

Contents

Difficulties on Theory
Inheritance _____ 11
Abandon _____ 13
All Lies _____ 14
Faith _____ 16
Stigma _____ 17
Sacrifice _____ 19
Harvest _____ 21
From the Gods _____ 22
Second String _____ 23
Mercy _____ 24

Variations under Domestication
Mother Day _____ 27
Gravid _____ 28
Mother Knows _____ 29
Catch _____ 30
The Home Team _____ 31
What you ask of me is news _____ 32
Martin Buber, Where Art Thou? _____ 34
Bird's Eye View _____ 35
Housework _____ 36
Measures and Waits _____ 37

Struggle for Existence
Grail _____ 41
Creation _____ 42
If at first _____ 43
Inventory _____ 44
For Submission _____ 45
Writer's Block _____ 46
Without a Legend _____ 47
Driving _____ 48
I Believe _____ 50
I Wonder about People Who Pray _____ 51
No Complaints _____ 52

Mutual Affinities

Are You Looking for Me? _____55
Maize _____56
Sowing _____57
Abilene _____58
Jazz at Sacred Grounds _____59
A Small-Breasted Woman Has Her Day _____60
Herbal Tea _____61
Red Signatures _____62
Guacamole _____63
green bananas _____64
false _____65

On the Imperfections of the Geological Record

The Last-Minute Catch _____69
I Gave It to Goodwill _____70
It Will Happen to You _____71
Making the Bed _____72
Competition _____73
you know you're getting old _____74
Beholden _____75
Unmended Fence _____76
Aftershock after Dark _____77
For the Death of Their Union _____78
Earthwalk _____80
That Other Person _____82
All Roads _____84
Counting _____85
Were They Good Years? _____86
Status Quo _____87

Variations under Nature

Reckless _____91
Thirst _____92
Turkey Talk _____94
Vogue Solution _____95
Eye Appeal _____96
Between the Power Lines _____97
And Hounds _____98
Circe _____99
For What Ails You _____100
Melting Pot _____101
Secondary Education _____102

Natural Selections

Family Album ____107
Bequest ____108
Natural Selection ____109
Vanishing Act ____110
Conservation of Matter and Energy ____112
Dinner at Dad's ____113
What He Forgot ____114
Tropical Bird in an Intemperate Climate ____115
Nothing from Zborov ____116
A Line of White Egrets Crosses the Clear Blue Sky ____118

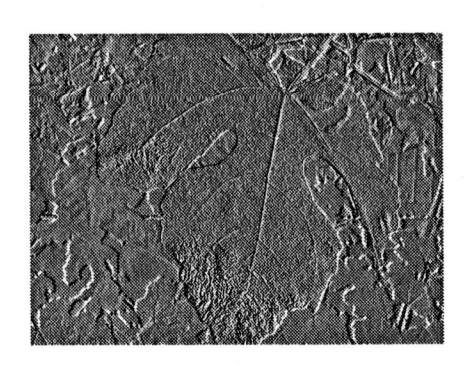

Difficulties on Theory

Inheritance

It was gluttony that did it.
Lust for the last drops of half and half.
The designers of this fine glass teapot
did not account for a woman on a Sunday morning
in a pique of thrift and thirst for cream
who would pour the last dregs of tea
into the carton instead of a cup,
and careful not to spill a drop,
but oblivious to the angle of the pot,
let the lid fall off.

I rescued it,
and with a smile at the close call,
replaced the still-intact top,
only to find on the counter
the broken nose of the spout.

My mother taught me
that china could break your heart.
She kept it locked in the hutch,
the dishes with names like Noritake
and Franciscan Ware,
and served us dinner on Melmac
she'd redeemed with Blue Chip Stamps.

I waited thirty years to buy this teapot.
I never pulled it from its high shelf,
or poured water in,
or washed and put it away
without thinking it might break.
And now, in the course
of trying to put together
the two pieces of broken glass,
I must have sliced
the inside of my thumb,
as well as here, behind the middle digit.

I'm tired of things made of breakable parts,
of the breakdown of the world,
of the fragility of dishes.
I'll tell my daughter of the dangers
of cuts and burns,
of stains that spread across best dresses
and heirloom tablecloths.

I'll warn her about appetites;
how cravings can cause recklessness;
how accidents happen when you're not careful;
how some things can't be fixed.
I'll teach her to drink tea from paper cups
she can toss away when she's done.
My daughter will inherit my mother's dishes.
I'll give her the key to the hutch, too.

Abandon

Outside the morning kitchen
a flock of golden finches
gathers in the honeysuckle.
In a week or two they'll be gone,
leaving the oblivious flowers
to the ruby-throated hummingbirds.

I never dreamed it could be like this:
red-tailed and yellow-breasted birds,
a touch of hands, a kiss on the neck,
a world beyond the blacks and grays
of common crows and drab sparrows,
beyond the cold efficiency
of too-busy parents.

Moon follows sun west past kitchen sink,
over branches of purple-leafed plum,
above the skylight in the hall,
and past my daughter's bedroom window.

I watch the days go by and wonder
how long before the finch will migrate,
how long the flowers will afflict my nose,
how long this gaudy spring will last,
how long this child will lie across my lap.

All Lies

I hate to watch the flow of blood.
I hate the red against skin
and the way hairs and freckles
become incidental.
The way things happen just by accident
and blood becomes everything.

I think Gunther belongs to me.
I keep him in my closet,
my sister's dog,
his boneless body with white floppy ears.
I'll never let my sister have him back.

"He's mine now," I tell her.
"Go to hell," I say.
"You left him and he's mine."
All the things she did
and thought
and loved.
They're mine.
I keep them.
The things my sister gave me,
and the things she didn't.

I keep the last sixteen candles
from her last birthday cake.
I keep her fortieth birthday.
I keep her children who will never be born.
I keep her yellow nightgown.
I keep her Judy Collins album.
I keep her broken-backed copy
of *Little Women* she borrowed from me
and never gave back.
I keep the people she loved
who loved her.
She was so selfish.
Everyone always said that about her
and not about me...
how she saved every nickel.

I hate her
and the blood going nowhere in her brain.
The long wait all day
and half the night

in the hospital lobby
with all those people
filled with hope.

I wish for her to be dead.
And for me to keep her brain
and her dog,
and a picture she made in 8th grade.
Now I'll put all her nickels in my bank,
save up for a teddy bear,
one with more stamina than Gunther,
who'd given up already.
One who will not just lie there
all limp and glassy-eyed.

Faith

Today, again, I'm grateful
for the red reflection
of the sunrise on the tiles of my shower,
for the sliver of moon
that reminds me of my miscarried child,
for the cool breeze
in the shade of the rusty awning
over the broken sidewalk
on the side of the building
leading out of work.

It's as if I believed.

Today again, my daughter
rides on a school bus,
plays softball in a different city,
walks home in the twilight.
She lets herself in with a house key,
eats a piece of devils food cake
with half a bag of potato chips,
and does her homework
by the light of the TV set.

When I get home,
she's in her room.
"How was your day?" I ask.
"Fine," she says.
"Can I come in?"
"No," she answers.
"Goodnight," I say
to the square of light
around the edge of her door.
"'Night," she says.

There is no cross on the wall,
no Star of David around my neck,
no house of worship on my list of stops.
So when I go to bed,
believing that tomorrow
she'll let me drive her to school,
and will come home again safely,
that is a real leap of faith.

Stigma

Girls are given names that encourage self-control,
good manners and sunny dispositions:
Rose.
Lily.
Names that speak of ancestral landscapes
and fragrance:
Heather.
Jasmine.
Even Iris, for our sexual proclivities
and our mothers' desire that we grow beautiful
but not wild.
Never Dandelion.
Never Clover.

My mother called me Margarita,
an optimistic name for a daisy
that grows abundantly in containers.
She didn't consider
that flowers sacrifice everything
for a short bloom above the damp concrete;
then fall back again, spent, invisible,
or forgotten.

My lover checks out the new neighbor in shorts
who pulls two panting beagles on tight leashes.
"Look at the bougainvillea,"
he tells me as he looks at her,
"the way the petals fade clear and papery."

I am transparent with this lack of attention.
I want his eye and his hand,
not just the predictable name
of our relationship.
Under my lacy dress, I swear,
I'm as wild as the weeds beneath his feet.

When I have daughters,
I will name them after stones:
Obsidian.
Granite.
Or for metals,
ones impervious to rust and decay:
Chromium.
Cobalt.

Nothing quiet or easy to ignore.
I will call them Lightning and Thunder,
Freedom,
Swift Bird of Prey,
Right Here Right Now.

Sacrifice

I've been dredging through boxes
dusty and redolent
of a particular mold
nurtured in the cool moisture
wafting through the garage window
cranked a quarter open
all of these years.

I pick up a picture frame,
blow dust from the smudged glass
and stare into the young face
of my brother in a stiff uniform,
resembling someone else's sibling,
a distant look in his eye.

Here is a pair of candlesticks,
an old theater program,
a sand dollar leaking sand,
a package of incense,
and a thin stack of letters,
the last ones from my sister
to me.

The same as any Mayan deity,
God demanded a sacrifice—
up the stony staircase to 6th floor west
where brains are split like geodes,
and rubber-tipped fingers
stunt the intricate crystal growth
of veins and arteries knotted red
like necklaces tangled
one through the next
and the next
unraveling red
until there was no red left.

There was a big earthquake that year.
And when we stood
at my sister's graveside a month later,
the ground shuddered again,
threatening to throw us all in,
rumbling with the outrage:
  Take her back

But the rabbi said
God needed his most precious jewel,
so there we left her,
there in the earth.

I had forgotten this picture.
I had forgotten these papers.
I had forgotten the faith
I buried along with my sister.
I dust off the things I want to keep.
The rest I carry to the curb.

Harvest

In our motel room we are five in a row
in beds made up green and orange
like the new toothbrushes we had to buy
having forgotten our own back home.

Four read and one pouts,
clapping hands on her belly,
unable to fall asleep with all this light
and talk and expectations for tomorrow.

She's hungry, she says.
I put down my book, tap my pillow.
She runs to my bed
and squeezes in beside me,
presses her head against my shoulder,
wiggles for a moment.
I am enough for her,

and I have enough
because I have hoed the past into my garden:
compost, leaf meal and sisters
spaded in and well-watered.
Nitrogen, phosphorous, potassium,
missed children and bellies only fat,
not pregnant. A rich blend.

At home I plant lettuce and squash,
corn by the south wall,
cauliflower near the garage,
and seeds for flowers.
Some sprout, some don't.

Weeds, for sure.
Oh, the weeds, for sure.

From the Gods

What fires do I bring that
headaches wake me before dawn?
I try to cure them
with the mountain of pillows
that proliferate on my bed,
hoping that sleep,
if it is possible,
or pressure
(if a ton of feathers
still weighs a ton)
will squeeze them out.
But nothing works.
Not needles in my palms,
and not medication
prescribed by the neurologist.
Only an anti-inflammatory,
an ironic name for the stomach eater,
gives me relief,
so I am like Prometheus then,
my entrails gnawed
by the vulture
whose vast wings
sweep away the demons at my crown,
and cool my fevered brow,
that I might sleep at last
to wake with my head
intact.

Second String

Rachel's not pitching again.
She could have been in right field
and she would have been happy
just to be in the game,
but the coach picked up a player
who hasn't touched a bat for two months.
His memory of her is perfect,
so Rachel's on the bench again,
and she's happy to go in as courtesy runner
for the new pitcher.

I remember when she used to play house.
Nikki was always the Mommy and said Mommy things.
Torey was always the Daddy, and said Daddy things.
Rachel was always the cat.
She said, "Meow, meow, meow."
And she was happy just to play.

Mercy

There is no mercy rule in life,
no time when after five innings
if you're behind by ten runs,
that the umpire decides
you've had enough. . .
even if you have energy,
and the will to go on,
and the possibility exists that a miracle
will let you make a comeback.

There is no time in real life when you are exempted
from further tantrums, from broken eggs,
from pinched fingers, bad movies,
moldy tomatoes and senseless commutes,
nightly flossing, chicken or pizza again,
useless remedies, insults and neglect.

There is no moment when someone finally says:
Go home.
You've done enough.
Get some rest.
Come back another day.

Variations under Domestication

Mother Day

Mother Day, unday of rest
no Sabbath but mandatory consumption—
me gift me eat pale back in the harness
love the child, me. Mother
the short-armed hands rock phantom cradle
that too real once swayed, two-footed

better the swish kiss and pass niceties
past cheeks of sag and ruin
all ripeness held side by
teacher's first-grade form
shrill the hard arms of armless chairs
everywhere no warmth but competence

back to the hearth and hostel
food and only clean pajamas,
towels halved and straight,
hands little mirrors slug
while bigger the ones chop
with infinite variety
the onions, chickens, eggs, livers

me eat pale back
in the harness
love the child,
me. Mother

Gravid

It's the end of May and all the mothers
are heavy with morning fog
and trips to school and baseball and dance.
We know that heat will follow soon,
and there will be no respite
from the kids, or the baking walls,
or our soles burning
on the asphalt.

By this time of year we are too ripe,
and greet each other with perfunctory hellos
and yell, impatient with the children who beg
for ice cream and cookies and candy,
but we offer only fresh fruit while they complain
as we drop things because our hands are so full,
so full of mother,
the other one inside,
the one we loved,
the one we have not forgiven,
the one we never really knew,
the one we see in ourselves.

Mother Knows

We had a tree in the backyard.
Every summer it bore only a few apricots,
mostly out of reach on the top branches.
My mother washed the ones that fell,
bird-pecked and smeared with droppings.
She cut away the ragged hole,
cut it smooth and shiny and wet.
It's all right, she said.
The birds know
which are the sweetest.

Catch

The other mother wants to know
if I catch for my daughter,
if I sit on a plastic bucket,
my hand protected by a layer of leather,
and trust that a ball thrown over 50 miles an hour
over a length of 40 feet
will lay itself perfectly in the glove
with a satisfying smack,
and that I'll lift it up
and lob it back to my daughter
whose hand will find
that spot the ball will hit.

But I tell her no.
I have a bad back.
I ditched PE for six years.
I swing like a girl
and close my eyes
when the ball comes to me.
I can't smooth my daughter's way,
show her the ropes
or even the steps.
I can't tell her
to place her foot
at a 45 degree angle
or follow through
so her fingertips touch
her chest by the heart
as she finishes off the pitch.

I know how to drive her to practice.
I know how to holler on the sidelines.
I know how to pay someone else
for her expertise.
My daughter and I walk to the car.
"Good day?" I say.
She nods.

Her squint,
the curl of her lip,
the angle of her chin.
Those I know how to catch.

The Home Team

The girls are tired, and stand in the outfield,
occasionally stretching an arm up or to the side
as the ball flies by.
They turn to watch it roll
towards the outfield fence.

The mothers, on the other hand,
are ready for competition,
ready to criticize the shortstop,
her ponytail,
her mother.
Second base.
Right field.
The coach.
The other coach.
What she said.
What he said.
The stats.
Hits. Runs. Errors.
Lies. Sabotage. Murder.

What you ask of me is news

and I have none to tell you.
Only the day-to-day routine
of breakfasts: English muffins
toasted not too crisp,
cream cheese, whipped,
and hot chocolate only warm
for children's lips are easily burned
and every cry swallows
more minutes than we have to spend
in these rushes to get to school on time;
of lunch boxes that have to be washed
of flavored yogurt
and crumbs from the corn chips
salted against the plastic sides,
and the container of yesterday's spaghetti
untouched but contaminated nevertheless
by time and temperature
and a roster of bacteria
and botulism breeding
between the napkin and straw;

of the bleating child so hungry,
there must be some Mommy-wrong
that keeps her unsatisfied;

of trips over the same road
twice a day
so the buildings begin to look strange,
and stopped at the signal
at Sepulveda and 8th,
at the corner of Supreme Paints,
El Pollo Loco,
and Champion Chevrolet,
I feel suddenly
I am in the wrong place.
The need to turn right
instead of left
rises up my legs,
pushes into my head,
so I check the rear view
to see if I might change lanes,
and oh, if only
the kids would stay quiet
we could drive north and north

and more north,
past the perimeter of our town,
past the long city
past the asphalt
and the tamed foliage,
and the speed limits
and the schedules,
into the wild,
wild ourselves
with this break from routine—

but when the light changes, I go straight,
and end up in the parking lot at the school
next to the same cars as yesterday
and tomorrow and this afternoon
when I pick the children up
and deal with snacks
and homework
and dinner
and baths
and toothbrushing
and stories.

My husband will be home tonight.
I don't have a lover to talk about.
A missed period. A rejection.
A new job. An old job.
An illness. A vacation.
I haven't been in a movie.
I haven't been to a movie
Nothing new
The same old stuff
Only I have to tell you:
I've had those things.
More, probably, than you can imagine
And I may not be a lively conversationalist,
but I'm one hell of a listener.

Martin Buber, Where Art Thou?

Once the child arrives, one's cosmology shrinks
to the size of two short legs and a howl,
and all the meaning, all the sense or lack of it,
has no point. Hand, shoulder,
peach-fuzzed head, lips to tit,
that's what matters.

After that, it's impossible to care
about symbols of logic
or metaphor.
It is the skinned knee,
the bumped head,
the baby-never-born
that encompass everything.

I baked a sweet bread this morning,
in the hope I could entice my child
to eat—to go out into the world
with what sustenance I could provide

This is my blood in the cake on a plate,
my hand brushed aside,
my words breaking against the slammed door.

Bird's Eye View

Let me tell you how it is:
a bird's nest of children
squawking open-mouthed,
endless grub line, fly and ladle.
Open eyes, open wings, always taking.
I'm talking about survival.

Father drags himself to work.
Mother is never enough—
my job is inside, in this cage.

Cat at the window looks for adventure.
That neighborhood Tom keeps me in.
Territorial markings waft over boundaries
and stick like graffiti to each stucco bump.
That cat thinks I was chattering at him.
I close my eyes for protection.
whistling in the dark,
but day or night, there is no cover.

My last wish
is that before the final bite,
my wings splinter in his throat,
these spears of calcium
press into the giving sack
of his stomach.

Cough it up,
cough it up,
it is stuck.

Housework

Hear the buzz of children
where golden-tailed pheasants
rise blind from the sofa
and leave me nothing
but horizontal dust.

Loose change jangles
in my folds and crevices.

Philodendrons and ferns
in their own struggle
between gravity and air
hide the dirt
in spider-infested corners.

I am tired of the vacuum.
This ritual of withdrawal
leaves me thoughtless, eyeless,
and visible only to those blood-sucking
gnats and mosquitos.
My torso sticks to the carpet
because there is no reason
for perpendicular.

And all the time,
those stiff-winged insects
light on my palms,
swaggering
in their egocentric ways.

Measures and Waits

I have learned my house well.
I have practiced door-locking
and the skill of looking
for the horizon through the eyes
of the windows. I know
the measure
of its floors
and its shallow breath.
I shorten my muscles
to fit the sofa
in front of the TV
and sit with the long shotgun
across my lap.

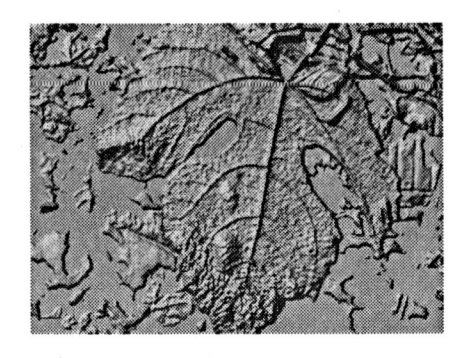

Struggle for Existence

Grail

I can't find the paper
I set aside for reference.
I lift every magazine
and set it down again,
every piece of mail to be sorted.

It's not in the key drawer
or under the blue sweater
draped on the couch,
not on the staircase
or between the newspapers
on the kitchen table,
not in the bookcase,
and still not in the drawer.

Even if I found the page I was looking for,
I wouldn't have enough time to read it,
or sufficient wits to understand
because the phone rings again
and there's no time
to find what's lost,
no time to set the house in order,
no time to sort the many selves
I've set aside for reference
along with the papers, ideas,
meanings and faith
I've misplaced, lost—
though all not so far away,
all just within reach.
There.
I know they are there.
Or here.
Where I've looked
so many times before.

Creation

When God created Adam,
was He just resting
or taking a coffee break,
having done the heavy work first:
light and dark, heavens and earth,
swimmers and fliers and creepers?

Was God just sitting there, I wonder,
noodling in the dirt with a stick
tossing out a rock here, a few pebbles there,
squeezing a fistul of dust,
rolling it over palm and fingers,
each grain absorbing the warmth of His flesh
and imparting to His hand the coolness
of the exposed earth?

Did He add a little water
and notice the change of texture,
knead and punch
some of it hard for bones,
softer for muscles?
Maybe He got a little carried away,
proud even, when He saw the results
of those knees and elbows,
and the malleable appendages:
noses, ears, genitalia.

The number five was good.
Yes, five on each hand and foot.
And twos, eyes, ears, breasts, nostrils,
symmetry approached not measured,
God having left his ruler in his other overalls.

I know that when *adama*, earth,
was transformed into Adam,
there was no one else around.
Had there been a team of observers
with suggestions for improvements,
or someone more experienced
with generously offered constructive criticism,
God might have given up, thrown Adam back in the dirt,
snuffed him out like a cigarette with the toe of his shoe,
declared the world finished in five days,
and sat back, beer in hand, to enjoy a long weekend.

If at first

This plant in the corner
of the therapist's office,
verdant bamboo—
grass with a thyroid condition—
telescopes its way to the acoustic ceiling
where it bends over
and keeps pushing up
when there is no up,
no space,
just a bending of the neck
a shrinking of leaves
its reach for open sky
thwarted and unproductive
a push
a push

Inventory

I want to write about nipples.
About nipples and doorbells,
but a girl at the next table is talking
about wetsuits and dry suits and underwear.
I want to write about things
sucked and thumbed
and travel on the other side
to France, maybe,
and Malaysia and Thailand and Africa.
I wish she'd shut up.

Nipples and doorbells.
And here is the problem:
even though the nipple
is attached to a breast,
and the breast is attached
to a torso,
to a woman,
to a woman with a name,
somehow it is not the woman
who is kissed,
who is cupped in one hand,
whose belly is traced.
It is not her clavicle tongued,
her ribs counted,
the transmission is shot
and have you seen the turbocharged
a list of discrete components,
and whether we call it nipple or breast,
we don't call it me.
Me with a name
on the couch with the remote
ignoring everything:
the mail, the dishes, the cat hair.
Me with the desire or the lack of it.
I name myself.

I am. All the body parts.
Flat tire,
dented fender,
piston and spark plug.
'92 Astrovan.
Toes, neck, knees, vulva.
Me.

For Submission

Checking my poem for errors
before I mail it off
I discover that it has forgotten its mascara,
that its pearl earrings don't match,
and that spaghetti sauce stains its shirt.

I darken its eyes,
find the errant earring,
change the shirt,
and place the poem in the envelope.

I lick the flap and stick it down
but once it's stuck,
I remember that I didn't check
for the SASE.

I weigh the thing in my hand.
It seems right, so I take it outside
and walk it to the corner mailbox,
slide it through the slot
and say goodbye.

When I get back to the house
I see a pair of black lace panties
on the desk.
I grab them and run out
to see the mailman driving away.
I wave the panties,
but he doesn't stop.

What good is the naked poem
without its panties,
the gift wrap, the promise
of more to come?
And when understanding is reached,
the slow discard of form and structure
that hides the poem
within the poem.

Writer's Block

Sometimes I think I'm a writer
the same way I'm Jewish.
Something I was born with,
a series of rituals I learned
and no longer practice,
a language I mastered
and have not forgotten,
an identity people respond to
that fills me with sadness
for the loss of its daily reality.
No mezuzah,
no Sh'ma,
no Shabbat,
no journal entry,
no first draft,
no perfect image.
Nothing tangible
to show for myself,
and nothing sacred.

Without a Legend

Chop sticks stuck through kimono sleeves
of the small figures on the shelf
wrapped in centuries of tradition.
Come into my black iris.
A red sun falls through seamed oceans,
binding us with traditions one-eyed and flat.

The promise of bread and drink
turns cement in the toes.
Baby legs, pins, prongs,
all the hooks swallowed.
There must be a new blue.
Dreams are distilled
into a chemistry predictable
along spoor-covered trails.

The comfort of latitude and longitude,
tick marks and degrees,
needles spelling out the convenient path.

The stars have been codified
into grids,
square, square
banked in some computer's brain
with no subconsious distractions
or fancy flights. The sure practicality
of metal and plastic.
Electric fans and automatic sprinklers.
All the fun is left out.

I miss my own childhood.
The fireworks of hoses splashed
on bald crab-grass earth
on hot summer sidewalks
and bare feet,
bone structure showing,
veins and pale skin so naked.
Another map,
another name,
another geography,
another bank of resources
a world to be discovered
without a key.

Driving

I leave my office
still trying to make sense
of work started and abandoned,
files opened every-which-way.
Order used to be easier.
Big spoons on the left,
little ones on the right,
forks in the middle.
"Dry them better," Grandma told me,
"and keep your knees together."

I read that a guillotined head
lives on for seven seconds—
that long to roll and consider that God has no faith,
people breeding willy-nilly,
lives half-finished,
and the records and filing system so compromised
there's no proof that one existed at all.
God worries
that man is his own invention—
that all the teeth-gnashing and prayer
are his own vanity
and he will live Eternity alone,
unneeded, obsolete.

Above the cars the sun backlights a bay of clouds,
a tropical storm blown north,
relief from the monotony of cloudless days.
Unlike this freeway,
my road is clear.
My mother will die,
and my father,
and my husband.
In the meantime,
the skin on my arms slips,
like sleeves.

I need to talk to someone.
I pick up my phone.
A box.
Hard.
Plastic.
Men create such regular things:
smooth, useful, compact.
Men manufacture.
I give birth.
I should have told my grandmother:
"Something beautiful will come from me.
Something irregular.
And soft.
And irritable."

The sky is getting dark.
I turn on the headlights
and flip open the mouthpiece of my phone.
I had an argument with my daughter
this morning.
Even now, after all these hours
she won't pick up,
and I don't want to hear
my own voice
on the answering machine.
I close the phone,
throw it onto the seat next to me,
and follow the tail lights of the car ahead.

I Believe

There is a package
of chocolate chips
in the freezer
that calls me
with its promise
of one
at a time,
like drops
of blood
or a single tankerful
of oil
in the vast ocean;
a little indiscretion,
a little loss,
a little spill,
all well within
the system's capacity
to heal,
hardly causing
a ripple
if you believe
promises.

I Wonder about People Who Pray

After the girl was tucked into bed for the night,
I wonder if her mother heard her calling.
I wonder if the mother turned down the TV,
got up from the couch,
walked down the hallway,
turned on the hall light,
and spoke quietly to her girl
from the doorway,
or if she sat down on the edge of the bed,
and brushed wisps of hair
from her daughter's forehead,
and held the glass while she gulped.
I wonder if her mother came,
or if that girl is still waiting.

No Complaints

My dad had a Jaguar
he polished with a chamoised
hand he never used on me
in love or anger.

But that car was so
sensitive it required
tuning at every turn

so he got rid of it.

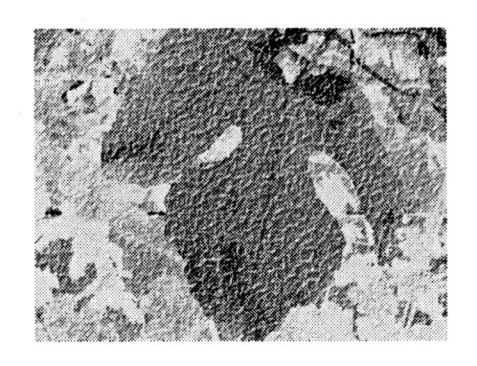

Mutual Affinities

Are You Looking for Me?

Sitting here in Lizzie's Cup o' Joe
I stuff down a bagel and cream cheese
before work, but what I really want
is for my old friend Ginny
(who calls herself Virginia, now)
to show up, as she did
the first time I came here.

The familiarity of her features,
the recall of her name, that name a question,
her recognition in return,
the offering of one's own name,
the number of years passed,
the standing up and leaning forward,
the hug, the pulling back,
the how are you,
the irrelevance of subsequent children or lovers
in the search for confirmation of the past,
of the life we used to lead.

I'm waiting for Ginny, and Joyce and Shelley,
and Nancy and Nancy and Shirley,
and Miriam and Claire and Yvonne.
I hope to run into them again,
so we can talk over a cup of coffee
and be glad for the encounter.
In the meantime, I'll crane my neck in lines,
search for the source of that familiar voice,
scrutinize the face of the woman
whose hair is pulled back with a jeweled barrette,
or that mom with a toddler heavy on one hip.
I'll wonder who that is
pinching grapes in the produce aisle
or buying shoes at Macy's.
And that woman at the corner station,
looking around as she fills her car,
I'll wonder if she sees me,
and if I remind her of someone she knew
a long time ago.

Mutual Affinities

Maize

Corn with a woman's name
lies decorative and dry
in my basket, a basket
woven like kernels,
at once rough and smooth;
its job merely ornamental now,
not functional.

Women do not age that way.
Oh yes, our teeth go black and spaced,
our skin feels like feathers
in spite of the ridges.
But no one peels back our clothes
and discards them husk-like
on the floor.
And our fruit's as hard
and pithy as advice.

If I could pry one kernel off this maize
and hold it between my cheek and gum,
it might soften
and fill my mouth with the tastes
of rows of corn with green and spiky leaves,
silk tassles gold and red,
waving in the wind for water,
enough to quench our thirsts.

Sowing

Rampant papyrus crowd the flower beds,
poke wild-headed stalks through the iron gate.
Older ones brown and fade until Wednesday's gardener
cuts them at the base, chopping with his sharp machete.

Still, along the ground, new knobs appear,
one after the next, following the green imperative
to expand until they hit the concrete perimeter
where they bend long necks over the edge
to shake out seeds with the slightest breeze.

The gardener carries a heavy sack
of grass clippings to the curb.
"Nice job," I say, raising my hand
to fluff my short, wavy hair.

Abilene

There was a fat boy down the street
named Charles or Walter,
I can't remember which,
and he lived in the grey house
behind birch trees that looked cool
even on the hottest summer day.
In an arrangement made by my girlfriend
who had to leave to do her chores,
he taught me to slow dance
on a sweltering afternoon in August,
his shirt dark and moist,
his face flushed,
and beads of sweat dotting his curly gold hair.
All our younger siblings were elsewhere
to spare us the humiliation of being seen.
So, without witnesses, he put the record on again,
lay my fingers across one vast palm,
set his other hand on my waist,
and I became nothing
but a connection between
his damp rosy hands,
my feet irrelevant
as he waltzed me
between the coffee table and the sofa
until Mom called me home for dinner.

Jazz at Sacred Grounds

Goz on sax
  ripe-and-pink-striped mango
with a horn
  she   they   music   move
and percussion strings drums
  travel my feet
    press my chest
      scales my spine

    a ladder climbs to the ceiling

    refineries on the wall smoke   (fine refineries on the wall)
      cylinders like drums
        blowing off
while a waiter poses bent in my ear
offering sweet and low
  no slide between syllables
only the dissonant hiss
  of the coffee machine

      Goz, blackbilled flamingo,
    beats in summertime
      snaps the sinew of the guitar
    drum flap of a thousand wings
      take-off of the flock
        and into the horn
  landing in rushes
    stepping up my estuaries
      salt-rich and brimming
        with pink-lipped shrimp

A Small-Breasted Woman Has Her Day

If I'd been blessed with wonderful breasts,
the kind that perked up a sweater
or even fit the darts of my cotton blouses;
if they'd been round and firm like oranges,
or poured, pendulous, into the cups of my bra;
if I'd had a cleavage
and worn décolletage with aplomb
that caught the eyes of all the boys,
as well as Mr. Harris, the chorus teacher,
then today, if my chin and ass are good examples,
they'd be heavy as my grandmother's,
and when not cantilevered high on my chest,
they'd swing down, nipples navel-high.
And I'd be looking at other women,
wishing for something less.

Herbal Tea

The dirty cups on the kitchen table
are tea-stained and empty
except for the last drops
on the bottom.

No tea leaves.
There is no fortune for me
that can be told from bits
of foliage.

What you need to know
can be contained in a paper pocket,
translucent, permeable,
wetter than you thought possible;
fragrant and subtly flavored.

Red Signatures

At the fair, among glass trinkets and wooden toys,
amid doily-wrapped knick-knacks and hand-woven shawls,
past ceramic bowls and tie-dye shirts,
a picture of a pine offers itself to a full moon.

The bough is arthritic and grasps
at the last few needles clinging to the end
of its branch. The night is blank,
without aspirations or stars.

Only a red signature counters
the black matte and frame.

This lithograph, corralled with other pines,
bamboos, chrysanthemums, moons,
itches in my forearms.
It is the one I will think of tomorrow,
the one I will regret not buying.

The one that makes me wonder what it is
about the bough of a pine and the moon
that calls me to stand at the window,
and think of pinning
a red hibiscus in my hair.

Guacamole

He comes home early
and kisses me
while I'm still
on the phone.
I've been eating
chips and guacamole
so now his lips on mine
taste like an exotic weed
sprouted in the daisies,
coiling toward a sunnier place,
tapping into my elements
so I can only nod
my hot-flowered head
and tell the caller
mm-hmm
to his irrelevant
question.

green bananas

green bananas
different from overripe
full cool skin and taut necks
no relation to the tepid browning fruit
its shriveling throat
and pungent sweet fill

false

my tooth hurts.
the one with no root
no nerve
a fake
resting hollow
on my gum
drawing heat
my body rejecting
not itself
but this other
with my shape
and color
and voice
and clothes
and smile
and age
and losses

On the Imperfections of the Geological Record

The Last-Minute Catch

Last night before he left for a late flight
my husband wrestled with the kids
down on hands and knees on the floor,
absorbing their leaps against his body
as if they held an energy he could store away
to keep him safe until he returned.

That's what I admired first about him—
a man who was a boy—
because I was never that kind of child,
the kind who could play.
For me there was no start
on equal footing,
no rolling on the ground,
no tag without a hit.

He's not home yet,
and I know one day he'll leave
and not return, in a rush out the door,
or slowly disappearing within the house.

I want to grow old with him,
and when he can no longer wrestle,
I want us to sit together
watching our children
play on the floor with their own children,
and us, on the couch,
remembering the touch
from child to parent,
from parent to child,
the longing, the wish, the flesh,
the knee, the arm, the calf,
the pulled punch, the hug,
the safe, the always, the knot.

I Gave It to Goodwill

He thinks it's still there,
that powder blue polyester minidress
with tiny flowers cut in the bodice
that I wore in 1970,
many pounds ago,
stained with butter
dripped from my scampi.

He thinks,
though I never try it on,
that it's still there,
that I wear it at night
when his eyes are closed,
when he's sleeping,
when I'm someone,
somewhere
else.

It Will Happen to You

Balloons the next day
that hover below shoulder height
instead of bouncing with a tick tick
against the ceiling
have their own
malleable attraction.

Making the Bed

My father would have said,
"You wanted to get married."
"You wanted to have children."
"You wanted to write this poem."
"You've made your bed, now lie in it."

But my mother knew better.
She knew that a bed, once made,
can be unmade, the sheets changed,
washed, thrown away, even.
One can sleep on the couch
or the floor,
or the back seat of a car.

She knew that sometimes
you have to trick yourself
into believing that a wait in line
at the grocery store
is a chance to rest,
or the slow drive up the 405
is a pleasure.

And she knew that sometimes
agreement, said with a smile,
is something else entirely.

Competition

Middle-aged housewives
sit in front of the TV on Saturday nights
watching movies about gangsters and warfare.
They go Sundays after church to the matinee
to see steamy sex performed by the young and lovely.
They come home, roast a chicken for the family,
and try to think of ways to lure the men
from the sports channels.
But life on the screen is so much easier—
sex smooth and mutual,
no calves pinched, no testicles forced
into uncompromising positions
requiring adjustment.
Games in reruns clipped and edited.
Volume up, volume down.
Channel up, channel down.
ESPN. ESPN 2. Fox Sports Net.

you know you're getting old

when the fingers of sleep
are preferable to hands
on your breasts
and you peel his off
and beg the others
to return

Beholden

The day starts out badly—no sex—
even though it's a long weekend.
Something's going on,
but no one says anything.
Her husband's in the recliner,
then he's somewhere else
without a word,
as if they are strangers in this house
with no one beholden to anyone else.
Nobody. No one. Anyone. Beholden.
A line-up of strangers.

Unmended Fence

Don't be neighbors with a dead man
whose retaining wall, yellowed
and dark-cracked like his teeth,
juts into the yard and pushes
earth and roots against our common edge.

He was dead before he died:
left deaf and spiritless by his old wife
who was swallowed by her own last cry.
Not quite lifeless,
her voice for months was muffled
under the wild ivy and scraggly junipers,
easy to neglect and difficult to tame.

When she finally went,
he got quiet.
No radio. No TV.
No singing in the shower.
No shower.
No washing.
No water.
Just the wait for her
to end this argument
and come up for air.
That's how they found him,
after some days:
ripe, and cockeyed
with expectation.

And now there's no one around for me to rail against
about the tilting of this wall.
My children and I mow our lawn,
pick snails, play freeze tag
under the shadow of a speculator's tidal wave
of new palms, poinsettia, and bougainvillea
poised on the horizon and ready to break
black-edged block and grain
over my head, and my children's,
spilling into our shoes
and under our flimsy clothes
till we relax from this task
of holding back the earth
and lie back under its slow lean.

Aftershock after Dark

I try to stay awake in the butter,
the yellow Yangtze running
sluggish in my veins,
the distraction of whiskers
on my collarbone,
of whispers in the howling face
of the moon,
the cackling of my house,
timber and plaster sparring
as night fog cools the pitch
of the eaves on their climb
to the nebulous red lights
of the water tower,
that ghostly feline rising
on eight legs, waiting to stomp
our stucco box
or descend for an embrace,
prone,
straddling the pools and trees
in its fatalistic response
to the shuddering earth.

For the Death of Their Union

Their aging house stands intact, condemned.
Its matted carpets are unseamed.
Where the mirror adhered to the wall
gummed splotches turn to rust.
The recyclables have been thrown away.

Even before the hammering began
the marriage splintered.
By final inspection
the wife couldn't remember his smile.

Her husband has a pinched tolerance,
a basset's muscled pace.
He's determined to maintain
his dour dedication to pain.

He's off the mark. He revels
in history's inevitable perverse drive
to repeat itself.
He never considered insurrection
from the bow-lipped family
in their framed perfection
held by a cross-taped nail
too weak for the weight
of this endeavor.

When his wife breaks with him
it's his mother's face he smashes.
An army of statistics,
the mildewed decrees of divorce
in leaky storage and forgotten letters
texture memories newly reconstructed.

The fantasies of bouncy girls
with their love for men
who in reality sag more matronly now;
thick-waisted
they burn over stoves
and figure calories and cream sauce.

He wanted only love.
No demands.
No children.
No edifice to be shared.

Demolition is soon.
Commitment of all the money.
In town, the bank holds the paper,
owns the old house
and the new,
the dream and the reality.
And when his wife leafs through the bills
the numbers of construction and divorce
balance and parallel.

Once they thought this house could make them happy.
They flirted with fantasy babies
swimming in endless summer aqua.

Now the husband stands at the back fence,
trying to see through to the water.
With his left hand, he thumbs
the keys around a key ring.
He bends down to pull a dandelion,
but leaves it in the flower bed.
Their house is gone.
Attorneys, like barracuda,
circle the bloody pool.

Earthwalk

When night turns gold to black
and branched silhouettes fade,
I slide into a tub of bubbles
to unstone my limbs, break the hold
of untrustworthy day.
        Evaporation and steam and clubbing streams
              hollow   I could be
      anyone waiting by the window.

Bats haphazard in my hair,
a cabin emerges,
defined in its geometric light.
Ill-tempered apparition, it stresses
the dark.
        Someone stands by a window.

Maybe a woman washing the dishes.
Maybe a man watching me
nearly naked in my almost skin
in the almost bath
at the frontier.
        A jackal stalks from the house,

a hyena eats the moon and I fall
into the jet stream seeking the equator.
I am not afraid.

I count stars, those angels' eyes
watching me from eons past perfect.
Singular. Remote.
They keep me safe in the night,
in my house,
in my self,
        because inside the pressure
of my own needles
is in the red
and fears perk up like pots on high

I trip myself.
In the night.
Over small cracks.
In the day to day.

    I need reassurance
because I am shrinking under the weight
of glass and concrete
as urban predators are forced into the hills
and I bubble, I spray, a watery sun,
day and night irrelevant in my mouth.

In the city, doors are locked,
plagues are fed to the ants for dinner,
God leaves for higher ground,
and clouds evaporate
as the earth is seared
under a cobalt dome.

That Other Person

Take away the child—
the meal, the bath,
the lap, the hug,
the necessity.
Take away the house—
the couch, the rug,
the dust, the armies of insects.
Take away the jobs.

I'll be underground.
A bulb waiting
for the cold to pass,
resting, gathering my strength.
I'm not nodding and listening,
for I have no chin.
Skid and squeal—
why, it's nothing more than adrenaline.
And I blame myself.

Blame myself for my foolish heart
with its rapid knocking,
for my underground existence,
for the dearth of air,
for this place of muted light,
a place roaring like the sea
pitched in a storm.
I'd give anything for something to see,
some vision,
enough for a headline.
And a voice,
even the raging voice,
because it's so still here,
and empty.

And I think, if only
I'd listened to my mother
and been more cheerful,
if only I had smiled more
and complained less,
if only I had followed that one rule
I can't even grasp well enough to write down,
why then I'd be fine, just fine,
held within this cloudless life.

I'd hold court at parties
and people would like me
for my silk and teeth,
and I would sing praises and hosannas
and split the world with my poetry.
Happy stuff.
The kind people would want to buy.
The kind I'd want to write,
the kind where mere paper and ink
generate their own light and roar.

I still tell this to myself
at night, under the covers
with my right hand on my belly,
kind of a pledge to my soul
through my stomach:
Tomorrow I will eat less.
Tomorrow I will exercise.
Tomorrow I will be that other person.

The next night I lie there,
changed not at all,
and curse my frailties
for their sabotage.
I take my hopes at the tips of my fingers,
under the heel of my palm,
in the space of the cup of my hand,
and carry myself into the dark.
I close my eyes
as the door shuts
on what is yet to come.

All Roads

For those who will be driving, the Adam's Mark
has direct access to all major interstates.

For those who will be flying, at some point
they will have to get out and walk.

For those who are wondering about the real Adam's mark,
the sweat of his brow leaves no permanent stain,
but his son, Cain, has a reserved suite.

For those who bear Adam's face
or Cain's mark, chances are
they were born of Eve.

For those who have pain in childbirth,
whose heel is vulnerable to the serpent,
gratuities will be given in the form of jewels,
but only if they arrive in uniform.

For those who delight in stories of clay and the breath of God,
they must realize that pre-registration
does not speed the check-out process.

For the 92% who believe in God,
good luck.

For the rest of you
sinners, heathens, pagans,
believers in false truths
and atheists—
I'll see you in hell.

Counting

I like being able to write big numbers.
The decades of my father's life.
The metal of my anniversary.
The ages of my children
(now twice my own mental age).

There's something pleasing
about the big numbers.
Even the years I've had this mole,
this wart, this pain.
As opposed to the meager number of days
I carried that baby.
Or the fewer than fingers and toes
of my sister's life.

Were They Good Years?

Did you bake cookies?
Did you slide down the curly slide?
Did you laugh until you peed your pants?
Did you dance with your sister?
Did you abandon self-consciousness?
Did you yell as loud as you could?
Did you skip fast and jump hedges?
Did you swing at the last pitch?
Did you have sex?
Did you know love?
Do they miss you?
Were they good years?

Status Quo

I've never been good at just leaving,
at opening the door and walking,
or driving away for the sake of driving;
or going down hills I know I'll have to climb
on the return.

Stewing.
Braising.
Searing.
Browning the onions
and sweating the meat.

Eating.
Eating everything
on the plate
That's what
I'm good at.

Variations under Nature

Reckless

I know about speeding
down the interstate with a guy
who wears sunglasses
over his horn-rims,
flying at 90 m.p.h. up the coast;

the search for fast food
and empty beds, the admission
of sleazy sex;

the abandonment
of the codes:
zip, area,
moral;

the redemption of orgasm
and the reunion
of alimony;

his kids
my kids
our kids
and the price of therapy.

It's not the wrath
of God that keeps me
at 65. It's the cost
of that damned
ticket.

Thirst

It's summer and it's hotter than hell.
My skin is the brown of Serengetti lions
and I am all spring and claw.
My husband has the speed of a cheetah
and that sideways look
behind half-closed eyes
that always lulls me
into submission.

There's been no rain here for a long time—
it's been all sleep and sex for months, now,
and I can't wait
for those droplets to hit the ground,
splash the dust,
and keep coming and coming
until there's no dry left,
until the watering hole becomes a lake,
until the mud fish unearth themselves
and come back to life
long enough to mate
in their clumsy, furtive way.

Diane vonFurstenberg once said
that making love with a husband
was like being touched by your own hand.
I admit to entertaining fantasies
about the hooves of zebras,
pocked by the imprint of gravel.
Or the enormous length of the elephant's
trunk I could lacerate in an instant,
right at the delicate tip,
the fleshy pink protuberance,
a little moist now
that he's aroused.

But I'm too enthralled by my big cat,
his endless demands.
Feed me.
Satisfy me.
That's all he wants.

I admit that some nights I'm tired
after bringing home an antelope,
harassing the rhino,
licking the cubs clean.
You'd think he'd give me a break
now and then.
But he never gives up.
And when he bites me on the neck
and growls into my ear, "How about
once more around the block?"
I'm ready to go.

Turkey Talk

Pink flesh. It looks fresh.
Naked. Like thighs peeled,
sliced, bloodless
on the sterile bed.
I tear off the wrapper,
reveal the textures of soft growth,
wave by tender wave.
First, a bath in egg.
Viscous, it adheres
then slips back
into the bowl.
Next, a ride on two fingers
and a thumb
into the flour.
It raises a cloud,
like steam.
Finally, into the skillet.
You know.
The sizzle.
The frenzy of bubbles
around the edges.
A turn practiced
on the tines of a fork,
quick and close to the pan
to avoid the hot spatter.
Afterwards, a new exterior,
tanned and appealing,
posed on porcelain,
the meat hot now,
more yielding
to the teeth
than before.

Vogue Solution

Let me be thin.
Let me be bone,
all bone and eyes,
a stick figure,
a suggestion,
smooth as a clothespin
easily clipped to a cuff
or stuck in a pocket.

Let me be thin as a junkie
or thin as my grandma
in her striped pajamas,
all false-teethed now;
thin enough to be swung
overhead.

Shaved down.
and pared,
like an apple,
like those bars of soap
we carved in Brownies.
Relentless
with the razor,
I slice off every hair
that pokes its head
out the door.

Leave me smooth
and soft.
Wrap my breasts,
in milky guaze
and cinch a silk scarf around my waist,
my shoulders, my neckline.
Pull it tight.

Eye Appeal

Julia Child is showing us how to cut a duck,
as if we have never twisted a leg or a wing
to find the joint—
or bent the breast forward to pop out the triangular bone,
or slid a knife between breast and back
at the easy point in the ribs.

"This duck is just lovely,"
she says in her funny voice,
as she reassembles it on a platter.

Give me sizzling birds baked or broiled
with crisp and righteous skin
of salt, of fat, of garlic-infused bite.
No flat potato chip,
but whole in the mouth.
Give me wing tips and chewable bones,
primitive in my hands,
greasing my chin.

I set the table.
Let others have the cutlery and dishes,
napkin rings and corn picks.
Let them eat dinner at six o'clock,
all the pieces that can be cut
into neat little bites.
They will never miss the neck,
the back, the tail, the liver, the heart.

Between the Power Lines

a pair of mourning doves
sit, indifferent to one another.
No contact. Just the glance
at his wings, at hers.
Not like last night,
their gray breasts red and hot in the sunset,
he nodding and bowing
until she agreed to something
that seemed like a good idea
at the time.

A drab male watching from a distant line,
whose bobbing was inadequate,
will eat his solitary meals
with no one to share the small talk
and trials of the day.

Today the love birds
sit like an old married couple,
courting rites in the past,
waiting for some interesting news
to surge through the wires.
Now they are tied, one way or another,
to a nest—
she to brooding,
he to providing—
and each believing the other
has a better deal.

And the singleton,
that one not desirable enough
for the continuation of the species?
He can stay up as late as he wants,
go for long flights,
or watch the other birds
without ever being scolded for his inattention.
He can do whatever he damned well pleases.

And Hounds

The man touches her.
She's put in a night guard,
to keep her teeth from grinding,
but that won't stop him.

This man and his chases,
all jump and clamber,
the bobbing arrow.
There's no sport in catching
the bitch who follows, big-eyed,
and panting at his heels.

Don't say how she watches him
drift into sleep, pink-skinned
and breathing through his mouth,
hands and feet twitching for purchase.

Don't say how she dreams him
all broken-fingered,
bent sticks and bloody dip:
raspberry sauce under chocolate cakes;
dreams savory aubergines
sliced through black skin;
dreams braised ducks' feet,
their slippery leather
sucked off softened bones.

Say that he loves the hunt.
Say that she is his best friend.
Say that she will follow him
to the bloody end.

Circe

She asks if my husband talks
when we make love. Hers only grunts

she says, and inhales, snorting and gasping,
kicking his feet like some drowning

pig. He eats with his hands,
chewing open-mouthed

her lovingly prepared dinner. He belches
and farts like a barnyard animal,

grabs her around the waist
and growls into her collarbone.

She shakes her head. She wanted
soft words and ribbons,

but holds in her hand the scepter
with a one-way switch.

For What Ails You

I cook a soup
with russets and sweet potatoes,
onions, carrots, parsley and garlic.
I boil them together with salt.
Salt is the key.
To soothe a red throat.
To bathe sore membranes.

I wash myself in broth.
Pour it in my ear.
Draw it into my bowels.
Cook and season my innards
to hide in the stuffing
the offal we throw away:
liver, heart, gizzard,
grief, anger, regret.

Melting Pot

Chopped liver is what we ate at home.
Chopped liver smeared on rye bread or pumpernickel.
Or eggs mashed with minced onions.
On special occasions, kishka,
intestines stuffed with spiced grains
and bound with shmaltz.

And yaprakes at Grandma's.
Grape leaves rolled around meat or rice,
and spinach-filled pastries.
Cheese and tomatoes and olives for breakfast.

At my friend Janet's house
we cooked baloney on a fork
over a burner on the stove
and ate it with mayonnaise
on Wonder Bread.

My children eat matza balls on Passover,
latkes at Chanukah,
McDonalds three times a week.

Secondary Education

I am the one watching, keeping, waiting.
I am the reason, when there is no reason.
"Read," I say, and they read.
"Add," I say, and they add.
Square roots square and unsquare in their heads.
I break the lesson down.
I cut it with a knife and fork.
"Eat," I say, and give them vertical angles.
"Eat," I say, as I push those parallel lines
down their throats.

But there is no eating.
Just the taste of arithmetic.
Addition.
Practice for multiplication.
A boy and a girl touch knees at one desk
floundering in the positives,
oblivious to the negatives.

No matter the process
I tell them
the steps
the repetition
the theorem
the bed

the chicken
the wipe-up
the congruence
the effort

the labor
the paradigm
the birth
the crash

the waste
the button
the platform
the postulate

the incense
the muscle
the sinew
the vertex

the workdays
the Thursdays
the lost steps
the catch

the track of the ball
the eye on the ball.
the ones who try
the ones who despair

the circumference
the trajectory
the sitting and doing
the children at the desk

the dog under the table
the scraps I give them
my plate
my arm.

Natural Selections

Family Album

Shoot a dream into the future.
Recreate scenes.
Airbrush stray hairs,
wrinkles,
peculiar habits.

These are the black-and-whites
I remember:
a crowd of children
in the bathtub,
in a wading pool,
by a waterfall,
their teeth bursting
with cheese,

and Mommy alone on the couch
with a wet rag on her head,
all worn out
from polishing
the floor,
the tables,
the children,
rendering them
blemish-free.

Photos are flat
so that
in retrospect
everything is smooth—
the teeth,
the skin, the day—
the red cheeks
a darker gray,
dry and glossy.

I take no pictures.
I leave everything
to memory.
No hostages.
No ransom.
No permanent record.
A convenient amnesia.

Bequest

My grandma used to wear heavy diamonds
which, year after year, pulled her earlobes down
with a long stretched hole
that left the gems at an awkward angle.
She wore a heavy gold chain around her neck
and a half-dozen hammered bracelets on her arm.
All her jewelry disappeared in the nursing home.
Maybe those workers deserved the gratuities
for bathing her, and feeding her, and talking to her.
But what did they say, holding the diamond and its back?
What words made her give them away,
plucked out from her flesh, the last things that were hers.

Natural Selection

It seems that giraffes would remember longer
than elephants, necks stretched
to hold the layers and waffle designs.
Stilts to lift and protect from peril,
sensuous lips to nibble tender leaves.
A perfect design.

No long memories.
No chains. No anklets.
No hard tusks. No rotting ivory.
No clandestine burial grounds.
And in the end, no faith,
no tradition,
and therefore no hope.

Just a folding
of bone upon bone,
shrink packaged
to return to point of origin
after a long run
on borrowed time.

Vanishing Act

The woman whose nickname means little bird
is losing things.
Hair color, body fat, gums,
mobility and continence.
She's lost the art of conversation
with those who are still alive and present.

Her house is dirty, rose walls now beige,
flowered paper smudged and lifting at the seams,
grout black around the edges of tub and sink.
Light bulbs here emit less light,
as if someone has thrown a handful of earth
over the house, its inhabitants, the car in the driveway.
Really, it's just the overgrown trees
in the back, and the new multi-story houses
that crowd around the old property.

The woman whose name means freedom
sits in a dark recliner, covered by a fringed shawl
that makes her look like she's disappearing.
Her voice seems to come from inside the chair.
"Cup of tea," she says again
to her son who stands in the doorway.
He goes into the kitchen, fixes the tea,
slices a piece of coffee cake.
"Here you go, Ma," he says.
She looks into his face
as he places the tea on a tray near her chair.
"Thank you, Good Uncle."
The reading lamp flickers.
"I'll have to fix that," he tells her.
"No matter," she says.

The old woman who has forgotten her own name
finishes her tea, then looks at a young woman
rocking a baby in her arms.
Her granddaughter bends down
to kiss the one she calls Grandmommy,
one heart-shaped face framed with brown hair,
the other with white.
"This is Felix," she tells her grandmother,
and places the baby on her lap.

Frances, that's her name,
grins a smile full of spaces—
her bridge no longer fits.
For a moment, the sun lifts itself over the trees.
Outside a jay perches on the windowsill,
checking for peanuts the woman used to leave.
Finding nothing it flies away.

"The baby looks like you," she tells her granddaughter,
"when you were little."
She bounces him once, twice, then stops.
As her hands release the infant,
the shawl slips from her shoulder,
"Here, let me help you with that,"
the son says, leaning over her chair.
She swats his hands away.
"Goodbye now," she tells him, and turns
to look at nothing that can be seen.

Conservation of Matter and Energy

Where did the neurons go
that sharpened her tongue and her wit?

What happened to the energy
and the gray matter,
for that matter?

What osmotic process
emptied the cells
of retort and memory,

so now instead of what's new
she asks—where did my sister go?
And my mother?
Where are they now?

Dinner at Dad's

I ask him to turn down the TV
so we can have a conversation over dinner.
Usually he does, glancing only occasionally
at the blank screen over my head
that offers no crawling headlines,
no Dow Jones up or down,
no prisoner led away in handcuffs,
no missing child smiling for the camera,
no commercials for investment bankers.
"Pass the salad, please," I say,
and he hands it over the platters
of brisket, potatoes, peas.
"So what's new?" he asks.
"Not much," I tell him.

What He Forgot

Today my father told me something
about his life as a boy in Poland.
That was unusual because he's spent all these years
trying to forget that life,
trying to be American,
trying to forget he had a mother,
trying to forget that he missed her,
and imagining himself into an adventure so compelling,
that it took sixty-five years
until he stopped and said,
"When I was a boy in Poland."
And he thought, but did not say,
When I was ten and came to America
I had a mother.
I was waiting for her to come.
I was waiting for the boat to sail.
I was saving for her fare.
I have enough money now.

Tropical Bird in an Intemperate Climate

My grandmother fled her cellar
covered in webs and dust.
She hid behind a pale mound of straw
at the foot of a muddy berm
and peered out from behind
a wormhole plank, to emerge
blinking in the fierce sunlight,
her heart beating rapid-fire
at the sight of so much sky
and at her first sun in years,
her first chance to stand,
to raise her arms,
to run.

She ran over the same fields
where her daughter had picked cornflowers,
where her son first rode a bike.
She ran to the green-banked river,
its waters singing still,
full of years laughing
over jumbled rocks.

She ran as the bullets pulled
like her distant children:
at the arm,
at the thigh,
at the cheek,
at the breast.

And as she slid to the ground
she gave a cry
like the shriek of green and blue parrots
escaped.
Loud enough to startle the soldiers
in their trenches,
and to scatter the sparrows
from the trees.

Nothing from Zborov

I told my father I might have to go someday
and visit Zborov, a little town
that was sometimes in Russia,
sometimes in Poland.

I told him I wanted to see
if the meadows are still there
where my aunt hid in the tall grasses
watching bees in the cornflowers,
and where she practiced the songs
of the wild birds.

Or if the street is still unpaved
and if their thatched-roof house survived,
built windowless into a crater
from a bomb dropped in World War I
which neatly excavated down to bedrock
a room-sized foundation.

I want to see if anything remains
that was good for my grandmother.
A curtain,
a skillet,
a button,
a book,
a letter.

I ask my father what he remembered.
He looks down for a moment.
"A bed," he says, "There was only one bed
in the middle of the room.
A chamber pot in an alcove.
A barrel of water outdoors.
The brick hearth."
He looks at his TV set,
at his city view,
at the collections of family photos
crowding the walls and shelves.
"Nothing," he says.
"There is nothing I want from Zborov.
Nothing was good."
Not the big boys who followed him home.
Not the stores that refused to hire Jews.
Not the shack where his mother sold beans and potatoes.

Not the year he missed school because he had no shoes.
"We were so poor," he says,
looking past me,
"so poor you can't imagine."

All this time I worried he was in danger of forgetting.
All this time he was afraid he might remember.

A Line of White Egrets Crosses the Clear Blue Sky

I am fickle.
I have no loyalty to color and line.
Catch me any day,
and offer me green, say,
and I want it.
Orange.
I'll take it.
Magenta.
Lime.
Puce.
Colors I can't remember the names of,
offer them to me
and I will go for them.

Or a trashy novel
a line of poetry
my own meanderings
a sporty convertible
the practical family car
a red wall
the white sofa
a pillow on the floor
a line of white egrets
a menacing formation of pelicans
a clear blue sky
a damned gray one.

I'll follow their trails.
I'll accept their truths.
I have no loyalty
to color and line.
I want them all.

Printed in the United States
23608LVS00007BB/112-624